My Mother, My Friend, My Child: Life Before and After Alzheimer's

Carmie Renda

Copyright © 2014 by Carmie Renda

All rights reserved. This book or any portion thereof may not be reproduced or used in any manner whatsoever without the express written permission of the publisher except for the use of brief quotations in a book review or scholarly journal.

ISBN: 978-1-312-19641-4

First Printing: 2014

Acknowledgements

Thanks to all my friends and family.
Without your encouragement, this book would not have happened.
Special thanks to Sandy Deyoe and Dr. Joan Roberts for help in editing my writing.

Mary Rose Renda

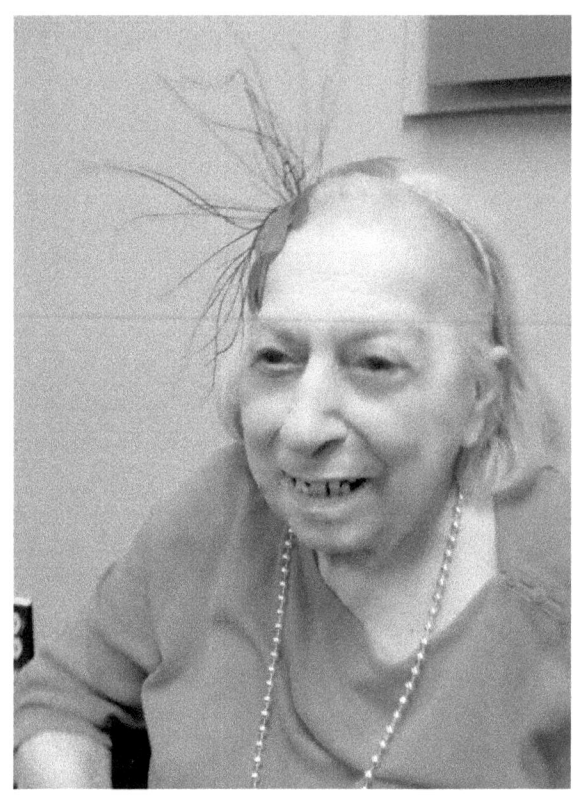

Your Mother is always with you.

She's the whisper of the leaves as you walk down the street.

She's the smell of certain foods you remember, flowers you pick, and perfume she wore.

She's the cool hand on your brow when you're not feeling well.

She's your breath in the air on a cold winter's day, the sound of the rain that lulls you to sleep, the colors of the rainbow.

She is Christmas morning.

Your Mother lives inside your laughter and she is crystallized in every teardrop.

A Mother shows every emotion… happiness, sadness, fear, jealousy, anger, helplessness, excitement, joy, sorrow … and all the while, hoping and praying that you will only know the good feelings in life.

She is the place you came from, your first home, and she's the map you follow with every step you take.

She's your first love, your first friend, even your first enemy, but nothing on earth can separate you…

NOT TIME… NOT SPACE… NOT EVEN DEATH…

Author Unknown

Preface

This book originated in the winter of 2010 when I was home alone with my beautiful mother, Mary Rose Renda, who has Alzheimer's disease. After the first day of being with my mother, I decided to keep a journal.

Let me just say up front that there is nothing funny about Alzheimer's disease. The journal I kept is written in humor, but in no way do I feel the disease is funny.

As I was writing about the first day, I realized that my friends might enjoy reading about my days of adventure. I emailed some of them. They loved it and encouraged me to keep writing and sending the daily updates. Others found it so entertaining that they forwarded my journal to their friends. Soon, I had people asking me to be added to my daily updates of what I called *Home Alone with Mom*. Some encouraged me to write this book.

As many as five million Americans have been diagnosed and are living with Alzheimer's. This number will triple in fifteen years. This disease is real and has no boundaries. I hope and pray every day there will be a cure or preventative drug for this disease soon.

There has been new testing but nothing has been found to help Alzheimer's patients. I recently saw a segment on CNN about Dementia Village, a very large facility in the Netherlands. It is a little city within a city and is the only one of its kind in the world. Dementia Village has two staff members to every patient. They can walk and interact much like we do in our own cities. If you would like to view this, go to www.cnn.com and search for "dementia village."

Before our mother was diagnosed with Alzheimer's, we knew little about the disease. We now have a better understanding of what she felt and how she coped in the beginning. Watching the progression of this disease is dreadful.

I consider us to be one of the lucky families. My mother cannot remember my name or if I am her child. However, my mom has been very blessed. For the most part, she does not display anger and agitation. Some families have to deal with cursing, hitting and terrible rages. On most days, my mother is very pleasant and happy. Mom never smoked or drank; she ate healthy and exercised. Mom worked into her mid-seventies. I remember my mother at my age. She worked and took care of everyone much like I do every day. No one can really know what it is like to care for a loved one with this disease unless they have been through the daily care taking.

I often wonder if I will be struck by this horrible disease. I look for signs of the disease in myself daily. If I forget something or do something a little strange, I think this must be the start of the road to nowhere. Knowing how active and healthy my mother was, the idea of me getting Alzheimer's disease is too much to even think about. My mother's mother, Nana Pigneri also suffered with this disease. From what I have read and learned about the disease, there is a possibility that it is genetic.

Many things have impacted my life of 66 years. Being my mother's child has been a true learning experience. My mother was and is a great influence on me. From birth, my mother taught me many things. She is still teaching me every day.

My mother having Alzheimer's disease has taught me what unconditional love truly means. I can only compare this love to the love you have for a tiny baby--a baby who depends on you for everything. When I look into my mom's eyes, I wonder what she is thinking and if she feels safe, much like you look into a tiny baby's eyes. Mom and I have gone full circle. When I was tiny, she cared and protected me. As a young adult, I considered her my best friend. Now in her later years, I'm her protector. She is my child.

In this book I have tried to capture how my mother went from being my mother to my best friend to my child. Because of my experiences with my mother, my heart goes out to all children, wives, husbands and caretakers of Alzheimer's patients.

May God bless us and help us find a cure for Alzheimer's disease.

Carmie

Ginny Renda, Marilyn Chiodo, and Mom

My sister Ginny and cousin Marilyn rent a condominium in Florida for a few months each winter. Marilyn is like a sister to Ginny and me. Ginny and Marilyn are always together, and Marilyn has helped with Mom for years.

Ginny and Marilyn drive so they can have a car while visiting. Every year, they pack up their most favorite things and hit the road. Until January 2010, this always included my mother Mary.

When they were getting ready for their voyage to Florida in 2010, I had a great idea. I would give Ginny a much-deserved break. I would care for Mom for a few days and fly her down to Florida the end of January. Boy, did I have a rude awakening! I didn't realize how much my sister did for Mom every day.

To capture Mom's entire life story here, both before and after Alzheimer's, I've mixed in my journal, *Home Alone with Mom* -- from those ten days together in 2010 -- with stories from her life in Des Moines.

Day One

Wednesday, January 13, 2010

Ginny and Marilyn leave for Florida. I'm home alone with Mom until January 22 when I will fly her to Florida.

I left my office at Bankers Trust 4:30 p.m. to pick Mom up from school. "School" is what we call Wesley Acres Adult Day Care when speaking to Mom. When I arrived at Day Care, Mom was in a great mood. Wow! I'm thinking this is not going to be so bad.

I arrive home. Ginny had made a lovely roast before she left. I can smell it when we come in the door. I put Zoe, one of our little baby dogs, outside and take Mom potty. I wash her hands and face. Mom is still in a great mood. I put Mom in her chair. I tell her to stay in her chair while I go downstairs to make some veggies to go with the roast. I'm not downstairs for two minutes and I can hear Mom shutting doors and moving around. "Why?" I ask myself. "I have no idea," I answer myself.

Calling to Mom from downstairs, I ask her what she is doing. Of course I get no answer. She has chosen to ignore me. I go upstairs and she is busy putting things away. God only knows where she was stashing the dishes. I decide this is not going to work. I take the veggies upstairs to cook, and put Mom back in her chair. I look over and she is taking a little nap.

Great! I have time to run downstairs and get my clothes ready for work tomorrow. The race is on. How fast can I get everything together? 10 minutes. It is a record. It only took me 5 minutes. Great, she is still napping. I pour myself a little happy juice (scotch and water) and continue with dinner.

Dinner looks great. I make Mom a plate and get mine ready. Go over to Mom's chair and wake her. Oh! She wakes up as a different person. Her truck driver side has come out. Hates this house, wants to go home, does not want to eat, and hates this sh*t. I continue with my happy juice. I sing her a song. She still is not happy. I try to get her in a better mood. I tell Mom how pretty and nice she is. She is not buying any of my schmoozing. Mom helps me clean up the kitchen, not saying very much. She appears to be in her own little world somewhere.

I put Mom in her chair and she keeps doing the jack-in-the-box thing. She gets up. I put her down. She gets up. I put her down. Over and over and over. I decide she is best sitting with me on the couch. I put her on the couch, put my legs over her and wrap us up in a blanket. Not long after, she is napping. She wakes up in a great mood. Loves me, and likes this place, very happy. The rest of the evening goes quite well.

The evening news is over and it's time for bed. I take Mom to get her ready for bed. This is where the real fun begins.

Mom has had, let's say, a very bad accident. I start the process of cleaning her and she has the need to HELP. HELP as in put her hands in IT. Oh My Jesus! Please help me! The stuff is everywhere. I'm dry heaving and I start singing church songs and keep repeating, "Jesus loves me, this I know" "OH Jesus, Please help me." I think I'm going to die and maybe wishing a little I would.

    I finally get Mom cleaned up and in bed. I take a shower and have some more happy juice. Thank God for happy juice. What will tomorrow bring??

Chapter One – Mom's youth

Mom's parents, Anthony and Francis Pigneri, were both from southern Italy. Before they met, my Nana Pigneri was living in New York City. My Papa Pigneri traveled from Des Moines to New York City to meet her. I think theirs was an arranged marriage. They married and moved to the west side of Des Moines.

Mom was born June 3, 1918. Mary Rose Pigneri was a first-generation American, the middle of six children. She had four sisters and one brother. All the sisters were tiny, pretty and petite. They grew up in a very close family, and all of them cared for each other.

John Pigneri, Mary Renda, Jessie Acri

Mom's brother John was the oldest. In most traditional Italian families, the oldest male child is the most honored of all the children, and he was known as the king.

Mom and three of her sisters, Jessie (Acri), Lucy (Scatino), and Rachael (Tantillo) were only a year or two apart in age. When they were young, all four sisters sometimes slept in the same bed. Mom's youngest sister Ginny (Bognanno) came along much later. Ginny-- the sixth child and youngest sister-- was fourteen years younger than my mother. My mother loved all her sisters, but Ginny was very special to Mom. My mom was a mother figure to my Aunt Ginny. She took very good care of Aunt Ginny, buying her pretty clothes, giving her dancing lessons and sending her to the best schools. She was my mom's princess.

Jessie Acri, Mary Renda, Rachael Tantillo, Lou Scatino

Mary Renda, Ginny Bognano

    In later years, Aunt Ginny helped us care for Mom. She had an unconditional love for my mother, and was always the life of the party. Upon her arrival, she could have a whole room in stitches laughing. She really knew how to work the room.

    The Pigneri home was on 26th Street, off of Center Street in Des Moines, Iowa. Papa Pigneri owned a building there with a grocery store on the main level and apartments upstairs. In the 1920s, this neighborhood was considered the "west side" of Des Moines and a very nice place to raise a family.

All the children went to St. John's Catholic School located at 19th and University Avenue. Mom would tell us stories of how they had to walk to school and home each day. When we complained about waiting outside in the cold for our ride to school, she would remind us that she walked to school and home no matter what the weather was.

When she was 16, my mother went to cosmetology school. At 17, she worked for a beauty salon making 25 cents per hairdo. Mom was a very hard worker, and before long, Papa Pigneri helped Mom open her first beauty shop in the building he owned at 26th and Center Street. She loved her work and kept her shop open until 1946 when my sister was born.

Mom and Aunt Rachael in front of Mom's first beauty shop -- Mary's Beauty Salon

Mom, her sisters, and brother got together all the time when I was growing up. Getting together in Italian families always included a large meal. My mom and aunts were fabulous cooks. They would all cook together and create a great dinner. The meal always included some type of pasta, red sauce, meatballs, fried chicken, and desserts of all kinds. After everyone had eaten, the adults would play cards and the kids would run around and have fun. We had many good times with my aunts, uncles and cousins.

Mom at a family dinner—aunts, uncles and cousins

My mother was a beautiful woman when she was young, with the skin of an angel and jet black hair. She was very petite. As a young adult, she weighed only 102 pounds. Mom's hair has turned gray, but her skin is still smooth like an angel, and she is still very beautiful.

Mom's mother, Frances Pigneri, was also very beautiful. Nana Pigneri, having lived in New York City before marrying my grandfather Tony Pigneri, had modern ideas.

Nana and Papa Pigneri

    She had her hair done, wore makeup, and did not wear the traditional black dresses like most of the older Italian woman on the south side of Des Moines. The older woman of the south side would talk nasty about Nana Pigneri among themselves; they did not like the fact that Nana Pigneri wore makeup, had her hair done and did not dress in black.

Day Two

Thursday, January 14, 2010

The morning went pretty good. Really nothing major to report.

I left work at 4:30 to pick Mom up at school.

Mom is in a great mood. We get home and I decide to wash her hair. Things went quite well. When I was washing her hair, she was sneezing and sneezing. Just like a good mommy, I took her upstairs and gave her some cold medicine. She ate a good dinner and did not complain.

While I was watching TV, Mom slept in her chair most of the evening. Of course, like a good mom, I was worried.

She woke from her nap and was still in a great mood. I brought Mom in the computer room, and she was as cute as can be. She could not give me enough hugs and kisses, trying to hold my hand all the time I'm on the computer. Oh what a feeling. My little girl doesn't know my name, but she loves me.

11 p.m. time for bed. Oh my, she has another present for me. This one is not like the night before. However, I have to ask the question, "How does a 4-foot-5-inch little person have so much stuff? Where does it come from?"

I get her cleaned up and put her to bed. Lots of kisses and hugs. She is such a good girl.

I thank everyone for all their encouraging emails. Special thanks to my friend Frank for bring dinner over.

Mom and Ginny have their bedrooms on the main floor. When Ginny is gone, I move upstairs to her bedroom. This, to me, is a supreme sacrifice.

On night one, I get absolutely no sleep. I have a feather bed that fits only me. My TV is on all night, and my electric blanket is on high. Ginny has a memory foam mattress which I find very uncomfortable. And of course, no TV. Disaster for someone like me.

The number one thing that sent me into a rage, around 2 a.m. I wake up. Ginny has these pillow cases. The kind we used in the 60's. The kind that are all silky. Your head keeps sliding off them. No matter where you put your head, it will not stay there. I have fixed the pillow problem with a nice pair of cotton pillow cases, and sleep was much better the second night. Still no TV.

Chapter Two – Dad's youth

My Dad, Anthony Joseph Renda

My mother Mary was from the west side of Des Moines, Iowa, and my father Anthony Joseph Renda was a South Des Moines Italian. For some reason most of the Italians settled on the south side, known as Little Italy. My father, who most people called Tut, was born in the United States on January 6, 1913 to my grandparents, Joseph and Carmella Renda. He was an only child.

As an only child, my father was very close to his cousins. The Ursanos -- Mary, Anthony and Katie -- were like sisters and a brother to my dad. Aunt Annie was my Papa Joe Renda's sister. Aunt Annie and my Nana Renda were like sisters. They lived about a block from each other in Little Italy, cooked together, and raised their children as sisters and brothers. I can remember going to Aunt Anne's for holiday dinners. All the cousins were there to play, and Aunt Annie's house was so much fun. All the kids would go to her second floor and play hide and seek. Her old home had the greatest hiding places.

We all grew up around each other on the southwest side of Des Moines. Aunt Annie's children married, and they had children. Some of us lived on the same street and played and went to school together.

My father was as handsome as they came. He stood 5 feet, 8 inches and was taller than most Italian men. He had very Italian facial features, but his personality was his strongest feature. If you had the pleasure of knowing him, you loved him.

Oh, how he could dance! Until he met my mother, Dad was a confirmed bachelor and had many beautiful women on his arm.

My mother and father met on a blind date through a mutual friend. It was love at first sight. Their courtship was mostly through the mail as my father was in the Navy and fighting in World War II.

Mom and Dad on their wedding day -- July 4, 1945

Mom was 27 years old and Dad was 32 when they married on July 4, 1945. In Mom's stories of her wedding day, it was a very hot summer day. Most of the wedding party was made up of young women as most of the men were at war. It was so hot that all the ice cream melted. Still, the wedding was beautiful, and the day was blessed. They were very much in love.

Mom had only been out of the state of Iowa a few times. Suddenly, she found herself in Virginia with my father waiting to be shipped out to some foreign land. My mother was very worried about my father and how she would return to Iowa.

Day Three

Friday, January 15, 2010

Morning started uneventful. I took Mom to school. Thank God for Wesley Acres Adult Day Care. I left work about 4 p.m. Not wanting to think about Saturday with no daycare. I pick up Mom. She is in a very good mood. On the ride home, I can tell Mom is doing something in the back seat. She has started this new grunting sound when she is working hard on something. I try to talk to her and ask her what she is doing. Nothing is always the answer.

When we arrive home, I open the car door to help her out and to my surprise Mom has put a pair of my walking socks on her hands. She holds her little hands up to show me her work. She is so darn cute! I ask, "Oh, are your hands cold?" She answers with one of her favorite sayings, "That's right."

Every Friday night is girls' night out. Any ladies who want to join us can. With Marilyn and Ginny out of town, it was a small group. Two of our friends, Karen Wiles and Fran Allen, went with Mom and me to Skip's, one of our favorite restaurants on the south side. As always, we see many friends and old neighbors. They all stop at our table to chat with us. Mom thinks she is at a party and everyone is there to see her. She is all smiles and tells everyone that stops how pretty they are. Our waitress was so kind to let us sit and visit.

We surely tried to solve all the problems of the world. We had a great time, and as always, the food was wonderful.

When we arrived home, Karen was kind enough to come in and visit until about 11 p.m. As Karen was leaving, I told her we were going to sleep until noon.

I put Mom to bed. She has a very bad cold and would not take her medicine. She said I should drink it. It tasted like sh*t. I'm wondering where this truck driver mouth has come from.

Chapter Three – Family life

In 1946, after the war was over, my sister Ginny was born. She would be always known as the first born. As I said before, this is a very important position in Italian families. She still holds this prestigious honor. My parents had two children: me and my sister, Ginny.

In 1948 our home was as far south as you could go. My dad bought the land and built my mother a beautiful three bedroom brick house on the corner of Glover and Jarvis on the southwest side of Des Moines.

My mother's first experiences on Glover Avenue were not all good. A street car went up and down our street, sometimes shaking the house. The streets were all dirt and turned to mud when it rained. There were no street lights. Mom used to talk about the move and how hard it was to keep the house clean, because there was mud everywhere. When we first moved, there were very few houses around us, although this quickly changed. Many of my father's friends and relatives bought land and built houses around us.

Our home -- 3417 Glover Avenue, Des Moines, Iowa

We grew up in this south side neighborhood full of Italian American families, including the Rendas, Randas, Rands, Ananias, Cataldos, Cardaros, Chiodos, Cardamones, Farrells, Leonedis, Tursis and Sodas. Most of us were related in some way and to this day we still call each other "cuz."

My mother always wanted us to look perfect. She dressed my sister and me up like little dolls every day. Her sisters and friends always remarked about how she kept us looking so cute and clean all day, every day.

Me (Carmie) and my sister, Ginny Renda

One afternoon my mom had to go to an appointment. I think we may have been three and five years old. My Nana Renda was not at home to watch us. My Aunt Lou Scatino offered to watch us. Aunt Lou lived out at Fort Des Moines, where servicemen and women were stationed during World War II. After the war, servicemen and their families could live there.

My Aunt Lou had two boys, Ralph and Sal. The boys were a few years older than Ginny. Mom had dressed us up in pretty little dresses, white socks, and black patent leather shoes. My Aunt looked at us, then at mom, and said, "Are you kidding me? How can they play dressed like that?"

Mom said we would be fine. Then mom told us to be good. Well, my Aunt Lou let us play outside and before long, the boys came and asked if we wanted to play cowboys. We had no idea what playing cowboys meant. They gave us guns and took us to their dirt cave to play. We played, making mud pies, and stacking them high.

Before long the battle began -- the girls against the boys. Mud pies were flying. We had so much fun! This was a kind of fun we had never experienced. After a few hours, my mom returned to find her little princesses covered with mud from head to toe. Mom was not pleased with us and less pleased with my Aunt Lou. I'm not sure, but I think my mom had some choice words for Aunt Lou.

Most of the neighborhood was Catholic, and my parents insisted we have a Catholic education. St. Anthony's Church and School are on the south side of Des Moines in the Little Italy neighborhood. Many children of Italian families grew up going to St. Anthony's School, and it holds a lot of history for my family. My father, Ginny, my children and I all went to St. Anthony's.

Most families had only one car, which the dads took to work. Because St. Anthony's was about three miles away from our neighborhood, the families got together and ordered a cab to take about eight of us children to and from St. Anthony's School. For about eight years, we had the same cab driver. Every day -- rain, sunshine or snow storms - Clifford was always there to take us to school and pick us up.

Waiting for our cab to take us to school

While we were at school, our stay-at-home moms cooked and cleaned, stopping to chat at the clotheslines, or having an afternoon lemonade or coffee.

Mom had the cleanest house in the neighborhood. It was always spotless. Mom's passion for cleaning went way beyond the norm. There was never a thing out of place. I can remember her weekly deep cleaning. Yes, I said *weekly*!

One of these duties included cleaning our kitchen floor. We had a large country kitchen. It was 24 by 24. Every week, Mom would get on her hands and knees and clean that floor. The poor little thing would start crying and tell me how she hated that floor. This went on for years. One day, I suggested she have someone come and help her with the cleaning if she hated it so much. Well, next thing I know, I came home from school and we had kitchen carpet. Problem solved!

Dusting, vacuuming and straightening up was an everyday thing. When we had sleepovers with our girlfriends, Mom would gather up all their underwear and put it in the wash. We had to warn them to hide anything they did not want to disappear!

To this day, she cannot stand to have anything out of place. My sister and I grew up with a lot of love, were well-fed and were always very clean, but Mom's obsession for having everything in order has never changed. Mom is still trying to keep things straightened up at Fleur Heights Care Center.

Mom loved to cook and always had friends and family over for holidays. She had a great talent for making something out of nothing. Friends would just drop in, and a dessert or something else good would just appear. I always was amazed at how Mom could go in the kitchen and whip up something to eat when we thought there was nothing in the house. Entertaining was her thing. She was always having guests to the house for fabulous dinners and desserts.

Mom, her father and mother, sisters, brother, nieces, nephews, Ginny and me

All through my childhood and even after I was married with children, Mom made pasta every Sunday and Thursday evening. Many of our friends knew they had an open invitation, and just showed up for a dish of pasta. In later years, my kids and their friends also came by to eat her delicious food. The number of people was never a problem. The more, the merrier! We ate, drank, and had many a great time at my mom's.

Mom's house with Dad's cousins

Ginny and I continued this tradition until Mom had to go to Fleur Heights Care Center. Now we get together once a month for birthdays of the month or holidays. Things change, and it's kind of sad. My kids and I really miss the weekly get together. They have very fond memories of my mother and her hospitality.

Along with her neighborhood friends-- Esther Anania, Edith Cataldo, Mary Tursi, and my aunts-- Mom would occasionally take the bus to downtown Des Moines to the Younker Brothers Department Store for the day. They went shopping and had lunch at the Younkers Tea Room. It was *the* place for all the ladies in Des Moines to get dressed up and go to lunch.

Sometimes, they would bring their well-behaved children, all dressed up for lunch. I was privileged to get to join them on occasion. This was such a treat for a little five year old girl. After lunch, if you were good, one of the workers would pass a large, beautiful basket with gifts. Some of the gifts were wrapped in pink and some in blue. All good little children could pick a gift from the basket before leaving. We all loved Younkers Tea Room.

*Back row: Ora Falbo, Anne Erickson, Edith Cataldo, Betty Lacava, Esther Anania,
Front Row: Mary Renda, Mary Tursi, and Betty Scarone*

    As my children grew up, we celebrated Mother's Day at the Tea Room. After my grandchildren came along, I took all of them to Dinner with Santa. There wasn't and maybe never will be another restaurant like Younkers Tea Room.

Jon, Mark and Gina Martin, Mom
Mother's Day -- Younkers Tea Room

Shopping was really a main event for the moms in the neighborhood. One day each year, downtown Des Moines had White Elephant Days. Oh, how Mom loved the White Elephant sales! White Elephant Day was the biggest shopping day of the year, and Mom and her friends never missed it. For thirty dollars, she could bring home huge sacks of clothes for her and her girls. Mom and her friends looked forward to this day all year. They saved their money all year for this shopping event and would plan their trip downtown for days.

Everyone was assigned a department or a store to go to. One would go to the swimsuit department, another to the sweater department, yet another to the shoes and the coats. Everyone would get their assigned department and grab all they could. On arriving home, they would lay out all their finds and everyone would pick out what they wanted. They had so much fun shopping, lunching, and coming home to pick out their treasures.

All the girls in the neighborhood sat and waited for the moms to arrive home so we could see what they had bought for us. As the years passed and the girls got older, we were invited to go along. It became an event we all looked forward to.

Summertime was the greatest. The kids in the neighborhood played outside all day, stopping only for lunch or dinner. Some days the moms made us picnic lunches, and all the kids would gather around our picnic table for lunch. I can still remember how much fun we had. The boys played baseball in an empty lot between our house and the Ananias'. The girls played house or school. On occasion, the boys and girls played together, with kick-the-can being a favorite. The only rule in the neighborhood was that when the street lights came on, you had better be home.

When I think of how far we have come with televisions, telephones, and other electronics, my mind often goes back to the mid-1950s. We were the first family on our block to get a black and white TV. All the neighbors came to see the new TV set, which could receive three channels. I remember thinking this was some kind of miracle.

Some of our favorite TV programs were *The Howdy Doody Show, I Love Lucy, The Ed Sullivan Show, Your Hit Parade* (my dad's favorite), and *Friday Night Fights* (my Papa Renda's favorite). Every now and then, we invited the neighbors in to watch a program. It was all great fun.

      We also had a telephone on what was called a party line. Our line was connected to our neighbors down the street. One day, Mom wanted to use the phone to call Dad. Every time she picked up the phone, the neighbor lady was talking on it. She got more and more frustrated. She remarked to no one in particular that the old bat should get off the phone. You guessed it! I went to the phone, picked it up, and said, "Get off the phone, you old bat!" Well, my Mom was so upset with me –and so was the neighbor lady – that I was sent to my room. This meant big trouble in our house.

Every kid in Des Moines loved going to Riverview Park back then. It was located off Sixth Avenue in the Oak Park Neighborhood. The park opened in the early 1900s. The park owner had been to New York City to visit Coney Island and loved Coney Island so much that he wanted to build an amusement park like it in Des Moines.

Riverview Park was located on a peninsula surrounded by lake water. You had to drive over a rickety old bridge. We would all put our hands in the air, raise our feet, and scream going over it. It had all kinds of rides and games: a roller coaster, a Ferris wheel, merry-go-round, Wild Mouse, the Tunnel of Love, Tea Cups, popcorn, candy, ice cream and more.

Riverview Park

Once in a while for a treat, Dad took us to Riverview Park. Those were good times I've never forgotten. One evening, I begged my dad to take us to Riverview Park. He said he would take us the next week. He said he'd get off work early and take us one afternoon. Every day, I asked him if this was the day. Finally, he said we could go the next day. I can remember being so excited that I could hardly contain myself.

The next morning, I woke up to rain. It rained all morning. I cried all morning. My mom told me she didn't think we could go unless it stopped raining. I went out on our porch and started praying and praying for the sun to shine. Soon, the rain stopped and the sun came out. Daddy came home and off we went for a wonderful afternoon. Such fun we had!

Riverview Park closed in the 1970s. Some of the rides, including the roller coaster, were moved to Adventureland Amusement Park in Altoona, Iowa.

My Dad and I were great friends. He would always baby me and whisper in my ear that I was his favorite. I'm sure he did the same thing to my sister. He was the greatest.

For a few years in my early childhood, Dad and Papa Pigneri had a grocery store in their building on Southwest Ninth and Jarvis Street, only a block away from our house. On a few occasions, I got very upset with my mom and her rules. I would tell her I was going to leave to see Dad and tell him how mean she was. Off I would go down the street to get spoiled by him! He'd put me up on the counter and give me a candy bar, and then he'd always tell me I'd better go home and tell my mom I was sorry. He always knew how to make thing right.

On Saturday afternoons, our moms walked us to the Holiday Theater. The Holiday Theater was located about two blocks from our house on Southwest Ninth Street and Caulder. The Holiday had Saturday matinees. Almost all the kids in the neighborhood went every Saturday. It was great fun to watch a movie on a big screen.

In the evening when the sun went down, our moms and dads sat outside and talked. Sometimes, the moms and kids took walks up to Southwest Ninth Street to the Dairy Queen for ice cream. Summer time was the best!

Day Four

Saturday, January 16, 2010

Around 7 a.m. I hear Mom trolling around. I go to investigate. What is she doing? I tell her it is too early to be trolling around. I put her in bed with me and the noises start. AHHH UMMM OHH GERR over and over. When did this start? What do these sounds mean? No matter what I say, she will not stop with the noises. By this time I'm awake and can't go back to sleep. I decide to get out of bed. I get up and all her little noises stop. She is then sound asleep without a peep and sleeps until 10 a.m. This is nice. I'm up and she is sleeping sound. I'm so tired.

My advice to Ginny and Marilyn: find a daycare in Florida. Unfortunately, the daycare would turn out to be a rehab center.

I started my day with not much sleep due to Mom's new out-of-body noise she started making at night. I gave Mom a nice bath and decided not shower because we would not be going anywhere.

Poor little girl has a really bad cold. We had planned to go out with Karen. I thought it was best to keep Mom home and let her get over this cold.

Mom was very quiet most of the day. Sleeping off and on. I tried to cheer her up with her favorite movie about Johnny Cash, *Walk the Line*. Mom and I watched this movie at least once a week, sometimes more. She loves the music, claps her hands and tries to sing the songs. Mom watched some of the movie.

One time when she was napping I tried to sneak to the bathroom. Mom's sixth sense kicked in. I hear her trolling. Oh please Dear Lord, what is she doing? I can hear her in the kitchen. Mom's sixth sense knows when you leave the room, even if she is sound asleep.

Going as fast as I can, I finish. Now anyone that comes to my home on a regular basis knows never ever leave your drinks unattended. You always must hide them. By the time I get back to the family room, maybe three minutes later, she has dumped my coffee, washed my cup and placed it somewhere. I still have not found my favorite cup.

Mom and I watch TV. She sleeps on and off all evening. At 11 p.m., I put Mom to bed. I'm ready for a new day.

The sound of silence is getting to me; hopefully, we can get out for a while tomorrow.

Chapter Four – Life after Dad

My mother and father were married for thirteen short years. My father died in a car accident at age 44, leaving Mom to raise my sister and me. I was only 10 years old, and my sister was 12.

I can still remember the day. It was a rainy, foggy Saturday in November 1958. My dad and I had breakfast together. I was his pride and joy. We talked and laughed through breakfast. He was telling me how we were going to watch TV and pop popcorn that evening. Dad left the house on a business trip. I went to a friend's birthday party in the afternoon.

Before the party was over, two of my aunts came to the party to pick me up. They brought me home and said my mom had something to tell me. When I went into the house, I found my mom in tears. She took me in the bedroom and told me my Daddy was not coming home. She said he had gone to heaven to be with Jesus. I just could not believe that he was never coming home. I never saw my Dad again.

At his funeral, the casket was closed because he was injured so badly. I always wondered if he was really in there. Sometimes I thought it was a mistake and that he was still coming home. What a tragedy. My family was never going to be the same.

My father was a wonderful, gentle, loving man who never knew a stranger. He really loved children. In the summertime, he might show up in the middle of the afternoon and take all the kids who wanted to go on a picnic and swimming. Daddy was the favorite dad of the neighborhood. He was so kind-hearted that on occasion Mom would get angry at him for spending too much money and time on all the neighbor kids.

My sister and I shared a bedroom. After my father's death, I worried that something was going to happen to my mother. My heart ached, and my dreams were nightmares. I would wake in the middle of the night crying and go to Mom's room to check on her. She'd ask me what was wrong. I would tell her about the bad dreams and how I worried about her. I could not sleep. She always let me join her in her bed. This went on for many years.

Mom was a stay-at-home mom until 1958. After my father's death, Mom opened a little beauty salon on Southwest Ninth Street in Des Moines. She called her beauty shop *Mary's Beauty Nook*. The little shop was tucked under the stairs of a building my mother and grandparents owned. It was truly a nook. She enjoyed going to work, and received great enjoyment from her work.

In 1966, I graduated from high school and went to cosmetology school. When I passed my boards, Mom let me come and work with her in the Beauty Nook. I married very young. After I had my children, I worked only three days a week. Mom and I had such great fun talking and laughing all day. I shared all my good days and my bad days with her. She was so understanding and loving. Mom became my best friend.

Me, Mom, Gina Martin

Mom's customers also became her friends. Her lady friends came to her shop every week. They all talked about their families and shared recipes. Mom would always come home and try each and every new recipe. She made many long-time friends in her little shop and worked until she was 70 years old.

Mom also cared for my father's parents, Joseph and Carmella Renda. Nana (Carmella) and Papa (Joseph) Renda lived with us in our home on Glover Avenue. Nana was a second mother to Ginny and me, and Papa was like a father to us. If Ginny and I wanted something special and my mom didn't have the money, Nana and Papa always came through. We were all that mattered to them. Nana and Papa lived to be in their late nineties. Mom cared for them as if they were her own parents.

Ginny, Nana, Papa, Me

Growing up, I spent a lot of time with my Nana Renda. She was a magnificent cook and taught me many Italian recipes. Her recipes really had no measurements. I learned her techniques by looking, tasting and feeling. To this day, my red pasta sauce is the way she taught me. I often went to her house to help her make her bread, homemade pasta and cookies.

To hold on to my Italian heritage and traditions, I still make these recipes for my family. During our times cooking together, Nana told me stories of Italy, always referred to as *the Old Country*. Nana spoke of her small southern village in Italy, its rolling hills, and her trips to the ocean. She talked about coming to America. She and Papa came together on a large boat with little sanitation, not knowing what the future would hold across the ocean. They made it to Des Moines, Iowa, where their relatives had settled. She was only eighteen and did not speak any English.

Nana always missed her family, and after my father was born, Nana became even more homesick. Papa told her she could go home to Italy for a visit. Nana made the trip back to Italy with her one year old son -- my dad. This "visit" lasted seven years. When she returned to Iowa, my father was eight years old.

Nana also talked about her family life in that small village town in southern Italy. Her mother and father were professional people. Her father owned a store, and her mother taught young women to sew. Her family had a cook and a housekeeper.

Coming to America was such a shock. In America, she had to do all of her own cooking, cleaning and sewing. Nana was a very intelligent woman, and she learned to speak and write in English. She worked in downtown Des Moines at many clothing stores as a tailor. Nana worked well into her seventies.

When Ginny and I grew up and moved away from home, Mom still had her lovely sisters. I understand why they were so close; I also have a wonderful relationship with my sister. Mom and all her sisters went out every Tuesday. Jessie (the oldest) or Ginny (the youngest) always drove.

Most Tuesdays they could be found at Southridge Mall, located on the south side of Des Moines, Iowa. They went to Bishop's Cafeteria for lunch and then did a little shopping. They really enjoyed each other. The five of them could break into laughter at any moment, laughing so much that some of them would lose control of their bladders. Everyone at the mall knew the sisters, and all the store salespeople enjoyed seeing the sisters every week.

Back Row: John Pigneri, Lou Scatino
Front Row: Rachael Tantillo, Jessi Acri, Mary Renda,
Ginny Bignano

On the way home, they'd stop at Dahl's Food Store on Fleur Drive for groceries. When they got home, all the bags would be mixed up. Everyone would go home with someone else's food. Mom would phone me, and I'd have to make a trip to one of my aunts' homes to sort the groceries.

If the sisters left the south side of Des Moines, you could bet they would be lost. On several occasions, they talked and laughed so much, they couldn't remember where they parked the car.

It was nearly 100 degrees the day the sisters decided to go to the Iowa State Fair. They didn't stay too long; they were just too hot. They went to the parking lot – where had they parked the car? They could not find my Aunt Jesse's car. They walked up and down all the rows of thousands of cars, looking and looking. After about an hour, Jessie just laid down on the ground, totally exhausted. She told the sisters she was not moving, and was going to die if they didn't get out of there. She said they should take a cab home. The sisters were beside themselves. Soon, a fair worker in a golf cart saw them and offered to help. Lucy and Rachael got into the golf cart with the nice worker man and went looking for the car. A short time later, they found the car and all was well. This would be their last trip to the Fair. They never went to the Iowa State Fair again.

On another adventure, the sisters went to the Val Air Ballroom in West Des Moines for a wedding reception. When they came out, it was about 9:30 p.m. It was a very dark night. Auntie Ginny was driving, got confused on directions, and turned the wrong way coming out of the Val Air. They drove for hours turning right and then left over and over. They ended up on Interstate 35 going south to Kansas City, Missouri. The sisters were very upset, crying, and then they'd break into laughter. They found their way home about 2 a.m. the next day. All was well. They never went out by themselves after dark again.

Mom and her sisters had many good times together. Mom's sisters and brother, John, have all passed. She used to be very sad about their passing and spoke of them frequently. In her present state of mind, she doesn't remember any of her family members, nor does she remember all the fun they had. This makes me very sad. I am lucky enough to remember some of the old times and write about them.

Day Five

Sunday, January 17, 2010

Mom had a really good day. I thought she was feeling better. No way of really knowing because she can't tell you. I cleaned her up. She looked real pretty. I took a shower. Of course, I had to bring her in the bathroom with me and set her down on the stool with a basket of clean towels to fold while I showered.

She folded the towels while I showered. I can hear her singing a song. She has the tune right. The words were all wrong. She is so darn cute. I listen really close, and she was trying to sing "You Are My Sunshine." I sing this song to her every night when I get her ready for bed.

This was the first time she asked about Ginny. My mom refers to Ginny as Jessie. Jessie was my mom's oldest sister who passed several years ago. She refers to me as Ginny or that girl. "That girl" is any female who is nice to her. She asked me where Ginny was and why she left her. Every now and then there is a spark of something real.

Karen Wiles picked us up at 2:30 p.m. for a late lunch. We went to Claxon's in Altoona, Iowa, for ribs and then to the casino to be a little naughty. It was fun. Won a little. That's always fun. Karen came in, and we visited and made some chocolate chip cookies. Yummy!

Put Mom to bed about 11: p.m. I went to bed about 11:30. At 12:30 a.m., I heard her trolling. Dear Jesus. I put her in bed with me. She was very sick. We were up all night talking, coughing and sneezing. I got absolutely no sleep. I hope she is better tomorrow.

Chapter Five – Family and the Compound

After I married in 1967, my family built a home next door to Mom. God blessed me with three wonderful children – Mark, Gina and Jon Martin. My children were my mother's only grandchildren. The sun rose and set with her grandchildren.

Gina Martin, Jon Martin, Mom, Mark Martin

We were a very close family in all regards. For me, living next to my mother was a dream come true. Mom became my best friend. She was always there for all of us. She would come to my house almost daily to help me clean, do laundry, cook and watch the children. I was very spoiled. Mom made sure my house was clean and my kids had everything they wanted. To top it off, Mom brought yummy treats to my house almost daily.

Most of my friends had to clean, cook and take care of their children by themselves. I had Mom. Some friends still remark that I was the only one they knew who never touched dirt.

In the last few years, the cleaning thing has changed. Oh, how I miss my mom cleaning up after me! I now know what it is like to touch dirt.

The Renda-Martin Family

My children loved Grandma Mary. Gina stayed with Mom almost nightly. At bedtime, she would say, "I need to call my grandma." Gina would ask Grandma Mary if she could come over to spend the night. Mom always told her to come on over, and off she went to get spoiled and spend the night.

Mom went to all my children's school functions and ball games. My children were her pride and joy. The only time I can remember Mom being angry with Mark was an evening when I was out, and Gina and Mark had an unsupervised party. Mom called me the next day to report that she thought Mark's girlfriend was running around in the street. It was really Gina. We never told her it was Gina. Mom thought her grandchildren were angels.

Mom -- very proud of her homemade birthday cake

Mom was not always mild-mannered. One time, she caught Jon and his little buddy smoking in her porch and chased them down the street with a broom. She was truly a second mother to my kids. Her love for family was second to none. Oh, how I wish she could remember all the great things she did! I could not have handpicked a better mom.

When Mark and Gina went to college and Jon was still at home, my sister and I decided to live together. Mom was getting to the point where she did not want to stay in her home alone anymore and did not like the idea of me not being next door. Ginny and I were going to her home two or three time a day, so we decided Mom should come live with us in our new home.

In 1990, my sister, Mom, Jon and I moved to the southwest side of Des Moines, just a little west of where we grew up. We refer to our home as the Renda Compound.

The Renda Compound is a gathering place for family and friends; our home is a large walk-out ranch with lots of rooms. Our home has two of everything: two kitchens, two family rooms and two laundry rooms. The lower level is a repeat of the upstairs.

We have raised children and grandchildren at the compound. We still host most holiday and birthday dinners. My children, grandchildren and their friends love to come to the Rendas for great Italian food. Just as Mom loved to cook and entertain at her home, we love to cook and entertain for friends and family at the Compound. Mom was always a part of all our gatherings. She is truly missed by all.

A *Gathering at the Renda Compound*

Day Six

Monday, January 18, 2010

This morning's bright spot -- I have a pair of Liz Claiborne black and white sandals that I call my slippers. I wear these slippers every single day when I'm home. They have been missing since day one. FOUND them this morning. Mom had hidden them under some pillows in Ginny's room. Yippee!

Mom did seem a little better this morning. I took her to Wesley for school. I have the day off. God bless this wonderful day.

I have the day to myself. My granddaughter, Emily, and I went for beauty day. I had a perm. Loved it. Emily had her hair cut. She liked her hair, too. This made me very happy.

Emily and I went to pick Mom up about 5 p.m. Mom was not feeling very good. When we arrived home she fell asleep in her chair and would not get up to eat dinner. Emily left around 7 p.m. I decided Mom needed more fluids. Every 15 minutes I would wake her and give her a little sugar water.

I talk to Ginny and Marilyn. They are in heaven. The place they rented is wonderful. I can't wait until Friday. Ginny suggested I should let Mom sleep in her chair for the night. Mom's chair is a really nice, soft, red chair with an ottoman.

I did get Mom to eat a little sandwich. About 10 p.m. I cleaned her up, put on her nightie, put her in her chair with lots of blankets, and made my bed on the couch. I checked on her about every hour. She did not cough as much as the night before.

Chapter Six – Alzheimer's arrives

Around 1995, our mother started showing signs of Alzheimer's disease. In the beginning we did not really think too much of her forgetfulness or her mood swings. Over the next five years, the forgetfulness and the mood swings got much worse.

From 2000 to 2010, we watched our mother change from Mom to our little girl. This has been a real role reversal. My sister Ginny did not have any children, and I think she always wanted a little girl. Back then, when speaking to Mom, or about Mom, Ginny sometimes referred to herself as Mama. I would often say to Ginny, "Well, you finally got your little girl."

Ginny retired from the Des Moines Public Schools in 2004 to care for Mom when she could no longer be left alone. Ginny has been Mom's 24 /7 caretaker. We both are very dedicated to Mom's care. Ginny has provided 95 percent of Mom's care for several years, with an occasional day off here or there.

My sister Ginny and Mom

Mom's youngest sister, our Auntie Ginny, was very helpful with mother. Auntie was always fun to be around and enjoyed being with our mother and our family. She could have you laughing within minutes of her arrival. Auntie had five wonderful children. All her children live outside Iowa, so we had Auntie to our home all the time. She would take care of Mom when Ginny and I went out for the evening together or traveled. God really blessed us with such a beautiful person. She was so good to us and our mother.

During that time, my mother would not leave the house. Mom was anxious and worried about everything. We first noticed it when Mom refused to go shopping or to the grocery store. I realized it was because she could not remember what she went to the store for. Even with a list, she could not remember where to find anything. I decided maybe I would take her with me to the grocery store, so we could do the shopping together.

On about the third trip, a real panic attack set in. Mom just stood there shaking, crying and insisted we leave immediately. This was my first experience with anyone having a panic attack. I could not fully understand this condition, and it frightened me. In the last few years I have experienced panic attacks. I wonder again if this is a sign of the disease in me.

At first I could not figure out why she stopped wanting to cook. She could not remember how to make pasta sauce, the same sauce she made for 60 + years. She could not remember what went into it, and even with me standing right next to her and helping her, panic would set in.

Total frustration was happening to all of us. Mom would get very upset with Ginny and me if we wanted her to do something she didn't want to do. She would go into a rage and scream, telling us we were no good. She sometimes told us she was going to call the sheriff and that he would put us in jail. Oh my, this was a very hard time for sure.

Not really knowing much about Alzheimer's, I was sent into a frenzy of looking up anything I could find on it. Mom has now gone through all of the stages of Alzheimer's disease.

Day Seven

Tuesday January 19, 2010

About 5 a.m. I heard Mom making grinding noises. I went over to see if she was ok. Oh my, her little rear had gotten between the chair and the ottoman. What to do? This could turn into a very bad situation. Somehow I managed to push the ottoman under her rear and pull her up. Poor little girl. Thank you God again.

I got her all ready for school. It took me a very long time to get her ready and out the door. Mom has a need to stop and touch everything and everyone on the way to anywhere.

Three more days. Hope Mom is better by Friday.

It has gotten to the point that leaving Mom unattended for even a few minutes can be a disaster. I personally do not leave her unless I think she is napping.

I think the medicine I'm giving her for her cold makes her very unstable and more confused.

I left work around 4 p.m. I was worried about my little girl.

We had plans to go to Latin King Restaurant with the Hawkeye Bank girls (girls I worked with a long time ago). I really miss seeing everyone. We have become family to each other.

I was not sure if I should take her. I decided she was OK to take. Mom and I met the girls for a lovely dinner. Mom was very pleasant. She seemed to be in her own little world. She didn't eat or drink very much. When we left the restaurant, Mom was so unstable the girls had to help me get her in the car.

I got her home, cleaned her up, put on her nightie, and put her in her chair to sleep for the night. Some coughing through the night. Not as much as the night before.

Chapter Seven – Living with Alzheimer's

Ginny and I talked for hours about what kind of treatment we should try for our mother. We took Mom to a geriatrics specialist. The doctor started a variety of tests to determine what was causing her problems. The sad conclusion was that Mom in fact had Alzheimer's. The doctor started her on a medication to slow the disease down. We were told there was no treatment to stop the process or make her better.

During that time, Mom trolled around at night dreaming there was a man in the house. Sometimes she wouldn't know where she was. She'd show up by my bed, crying and confused. I always put her in bed with me and gave her hugs and kisses. Who was this man? Her vivid dreams seemed so real. Why did this dream seem so true? These episodes just broke my heart.

On several occasions in the middle of the night, Mom opened the front door and set off the house alarm. Ginny and I always ran to the door to see what was going on. There would be Mom, just stunned. When asked where she was going, she would say she was going home or she just didn't know. To this day, we have no idea where "home" was. It might have been her home as a little girl or the home where she raised us. We are still not sure.

One day, I decided I would take her by the house where we were raised. Maybe that was "home"? When we got to the neighborhood, I stopped in front of our home and asked her if she remembered our house. She just stared out the window with a blank look on her face. Sadness took over my whole body. She had no idea where we were. How does fifty years disappear from one's mind?

We went on down the street to Southwest Ninth where Mom had her little beauty shop. Still nothing. How sad it was to see my little girl sitting in my car playing with her tissues. She did not recall any of the neighborhood.

Speech became a problem for Mom. This is another effect of Alzheimer's. We would be out for a drive in a lot of traffic and she would tell me how terrible all the trees were. What she really meant was there were a lot of cars. Today Mom does not speak in words. She now has her own language. We still pretend we know what she is saying although we have no idea.

Auntie Ginny became very ill, passing away in 2006. We all miss her very much. After her passing, we were left with no choice. Mom had to come with us whenever we were both going to be gone.

In the beginning, Mom would just refuse to go. One evening we had guests from out of town, friends my sister went to high school with. We got ready to go, and Mom would not move. She started screaming. That night I decided to stay home with Mom, and Ginny went to dinner with our friends. After that evening, we were very firm and told her she had no choice. She had to go with us from now on.

Out with friends

It was not long before Mom was waiting every day to go out, mostly with Ginny and our cousin Marilyn. Every day, Ginny got Mom up, bathed, fed and took her everywhere she went. Mom now wanted to go all the time. Every morning she would ask Ginny when they were going. Some days, they were not going anywhere and she would still ask a hundred times when they were leaving. Other times, she would just appear with her coat on.

An evening out with the old neighborhood

One afternoon Ginny had Book Club. As the ladies were leaving, Mom went and put her coat on, determined that she was going to go, too. My sister had to sit her down and tell her they had too much work to do. She needed to stay at home and help her clean up.

Without Ginny's knowledge, Mom would also go in the garage, get in the back seat of Ginny's van and sit and wait for Ginny. This would cause Ginny to frantically look for Mom. One afternoon I went downstairs and left Mom sleeping in her chair. When I returned upstairs, there was no Mom. Oh my God!

Where had she gone? When Ginny came out of her bedroom, I was in a panic. Ginny just went to the garage, and Mom was sitting in the backseat of the van waiting to go somewhere. Anywhere….

Mom and friends at a gala wedding

When Marilyn came over, Mom would go for her coat, put it on, and stand by the door waiting to go in the car. Mom wanted to go all the time. I would have to put Mom in the car and drive around the block so she thought she went someplace. In the last few years, we've not been able to leave Mom unattended for any length of time. When Mom wandered off, we called it "trolling."

Mom became part of our group of friends. Our group consists of any ladies wanting to go out on a Friday evening for dinner and lots of laughs. Our friends knew that an invitation to us included Mom. Mom is loved by all our friends – Mom refers to a lot of our friends as her best friends.

Whether hosting parties at the Renda Compound or going to a friend's home, one of our friends always sat with Mom, held her hand and talked to her. She then would look at them and say "You are my best friend." When friends come to visit, whether for an hour or a week, they always include Mom in whatever is going on. We are very blessed to have such good friends.

We also love to travel, going to Chicago, Las Vegas, Lake Tahoe, New York, Florida, Kansas City and the Lake of the Ozarks, just to name a few places. Mom was always with us wherever we went, except for an occasional night out when one of us would stay home with her.

During our travels in the last couple of years, we have taken Mom to see some great musicals. We took her to see *Wicked* in Chicago, Bette Midler in Las Vegas, *Jersey Boys* in Las Vegas and *The Lion King* in Des Moines. She loves all the excitement of the musicals.

Ginny Renda, Marilyn Chiodo, Me, Mom in Chicago

I think her favorite was *Wicked in Chicago*. We were right up front. She did not move a muscle except for a few times. Like all children, she was a little frightened of the flying monkeys. She clapped her hands to the music. Mom loves music of any kind.

Mom's favorite movie is *Walk the Line*. She loves the music, clapping and trying to sing along with June and Johnny Cash. We watched this movie at least once a week, sometimes more than once in a day.

Once in Las Vegas, we were getting ready to go to dinner. Our cousin Marilyn was in one bathroom, Ginny was in another bathroom, and I was in the bedroom getting dressed. Mom was napping in the sitting room. I came out of the bedroom and didn't see Mom. I yelled for Ginny and Marilyn. Mom was not with them. We were all frantic. We ran out the door and down the hall. There was Mom, waiting for the elevator. Thank God we caught her before she got on the elevator! When we caught her, we asked her where she was going. Her answer was "home." Sometimes even when we are at home, Mom will say she wants to go home.

Las Vegas 2006 -- Ginny, Marilyn, Mom, Me

After the Las Vegas incident, when I was in charge, I had her with me every minute. If I went to the bathroom, she went with me. If I went outside, she went with me. I would never leave her for more than a few minutes.

Ginny, being with Mom every day all day, was a little more trusting than I was. On occasion, Ginny would leave Mom alone for five or ten minutes, which sometimes would be a disaster. Mom was known to leave the house.

Once, Ginny was taking a shower. She had put Mom to work folding some towels in the same bathroom. Ginny could hear that Mom had left the room. "Mother? Mother?" No answer.

Mom has a way of ignoring you when she is on a mission. This time, she had decided to take a little walk. In no time, she was out the door and down the street. She didn't get too far. My granddaughter, Maria, was walking to our house after school and found Mom outside down the street. Maria brought her into the house just as Ginny was getting out of the shower to look for her.

After that adventure, we started setting the house alarms anytime we would leave her for more than five minutes, just in case Mom decided to troll.

Day Eight

Wednesday, January 20, 2010

Oh what a lovely morning. The morning comes with freezing rain, yippee! Ice everywhere.

When caring for your aging, memory-declining parent, you try to do the same thing at the same time in the same way. They hate any type of change.

I get Mom up to clean her up. She seems to be a little better. Here's the fun part of the morning. Anyone who cares for or has been around Alzheimer's patients will enjoy this.

After cleaning her up and dressing Mom, it is brush your teeth time. She stands at the sink and I brush her teeth. Then comes the Scope. I put a small amount of Scope in the cup and tell her to swish. She does a fine job.

I make the mistake of trying to give her cough medicine right after the swishing and spitting her mouth wash. She takes the cough medicine. I tell her to drink it. Oh No! She swishes and spits it out right on my hand.

I look at her sweet little face and very sweetly say, "Thank you." She looks at me and very sweetly says, "You're welcome."

I took Mom to school late – about 10:30 a.m. There was freezing rain and it was very cold out. There was only one other lady at Wesley. I desperately asked if it was ok to leave her and they said it would be fine.

I went to work and worked until about 2:30. I left work, went to the store to stock the refrigerator for Claude Boyle, my sister's friend. He will be staying with our little dog Zoe when Mom and I go to Florida tomorrow.

Picked up Mom. Denise, at Wesley Day Care, was very concerned about Mom's cough. She suggested I call the doctor. Who would think our little girl would get so sick she would need the doctor?

Ginny – and I need to say right now that she is a saint and should be canonized for caring for Mom all these years – but how could she leave town without writing any emergency information? No doctor, insurance or Medicare information. Note to all. Always write down emergency numbers and have them if needed.

The task of finding doctors' numbers, Medicare cards and drug cards (what task? Finding Ginny?) took me more than two hours.

The doctor was very kind and ordered an antibiotic. OK. Now, how do I get to Dahl's Pharmacy to pick this prescription up? I can't take Mom out in the ice storm. I called my good friend, Frank Swesey. He is so kind. He offers to go get the medicine.

Now anyone that knows me well knows I could be my own sitcom.

Knowing it is garbage night; I collect all the house waste, get the big brown garbage container outside and load it up. I am only 4-feet-11-inches tall, and the large brown container is about 4 feet tall.

I take a look at my driveway. This is not a pretty sight. My driveway is totally covered with about an inch of ice. Oh so carefully, I make my way down the driveway. I come to the end of the driveway, and down a small incline the can and I roll. I'm saying out loud "Oh God", "Oh God", "Help me please". It's a miracle I'm still standing.

When I turn to go back up the drive, I can see it's still not a good thing. I try to move forward. Bam! Down I go. I can't get up. Crying I crawling on all fours, I get to a small spot in the snow covered lawn where there is no ice. I finally make it back to the house.

This is not the end.

Our dog pen has a small opening from our porch, with three steps down, to the dog pen. I had previously opened the little door to let Zoe out in the pen. When I go to let Zoe in, she could not make it up the steps. She is slipping and sliding. The steps were covered with ice.

I try to get my 120 pound body through this 10 inch opening to the dog pen. I'm grabbing for her. I try and try to get her. No way. The little dog is at the bottom of the steps crying. Think! Think! Think!

I get some towels, throw them down on the steps, and finally get the poor little thing in the house.

Frank came with the antibiotic. We gave Mom a double dose as instructed by the doctor. She slept most of the night.

Another note to all: happy juice helps all situations.

Chapter Eight – New Challenges

In the spring of 2009, my sister Ginny became ill and was hospitalized. I had no idea what I was going to do with Mom while I worked. I thought Ginny would be ok in a couple of days and all would be good. I could do this if it was only a few days of dragging my little mommy all over with me.

I took Mom to work with me, which was quite a chore. I would get her up, clean her, and feed her breakfast. Then, I would pack a lunch and we'd head off to Bankers Trust, where I worked as a loan officer. I would give her papers to read. She would straighten out my desk and help with all sorts of duties.

Ginny's hospital stay turned out to be more than a couple of days. She was very ill and needed to be in intensive care. I had to find someone to care for Mom during the day. I called all sorts of organizations and was told it was going to be $25 to $30 an hour for in-home care. How could anyone afford these prices?

This is when I started to realize how much my sister was doing for my mom. In my search I found an adult day care for Mom. Wesley Adult Day Care is located on Grand Avenue on the west side of Des Moines. On my first call to Wesley, I was told they could put her on their waiting list, and it would most likely be a 6-month wait. I was shocked to find out there were so few facilities to care for the elderly. I explained my situation to Denise, the director. She was very kind and found Mom a spot. Wesley totally saved my life. I would then get Mom up and ready, take her to Wesley on Grand Ave. and go to work.

Of course in the beginning like a good mom, I would call to make sure Mom was doing ok. I would pick her up on my way home from work. What a blessing! I did not have to worry all day about her.

We referred to Wesley Adult Day Care as "school" when talking to Mom. Mom never said she didn't want to go to school. She really liked going. Ginny recovered, and realizing how much she had been doing every day, we decided to send Mom to school three days a week. Mom went to Wesley Day care for a year, and we knew Mom was in a very nice, safe and loving place.

As the disease progressed, dressing Mom became an adventure. Sometimes, she would go to her room and put on layers of clothing. The clothes would have no particular order. Panties and bras could be over her pants and shirts. Trying to get her to remove them was always a task.

Another time when Ginny was in the shower --my sister is a very clean person-- I had placed a 1970s outfit on Ginny's bed for my 12 year old granddaughter Maria. The outfit consisted of tight black leggings, five-inch black studded heels, and a long tunic. Mom decided the outfit must have been for her. Mom dressed herself in this outfit, heels and all, and waited for Ginny to come out of the shower. This was quite a sight. Ginny had a very hard time removing the tights and to this day is not sure how Mom was able to get them on.

As the years passed, Mom's Alzheimer's progressed and her mind started going back to childish ways. When my grandchildren visited, Mom would become jealous, wanting to know who they were, why they were there, and when they would be going home. She sometimes even told them to go home. I had to sit the kids down and explain why Grandma Mary was acting this way.

One day when my grandson Sean was over, Mom felt left out. At the time he was about five. He was playing and we were watching a movie. Every time Sean got a little too close to Mom, out came her foot with a little kick. I scolded her, told her she was being naughty and said it was not nice to kick little kids. Mom just looked at me and said she thought it was time for him to go home. I made her promise she would be a good girl. At this point, she wanted all my attention and wasn't going to share my time with anyone. After that incident, I had the grandchildren play in a different room.

One time in the middle of the night, Mom got up and decided to make Ginny's bed. Make the bed she did! Mom made that bed very tight. You could bounce a quarter on a bed that Mom made. All the sheets were tucked in perfectly. She put Ginny's 20 pillows on top, left the room, and tried to leave the house. Keep in mind-- Ginny was still in her bed. The sheets were pulled so tight that she could not find her way out of the bed. The house alarm was blaring. I ran up the stairs to find Mom at the front door. She looked like she was in shock. I looked at her and asked where Ginny was. She answered she didn't know. As I went into Ginny's room I could hear muffled sounds. I called out to her, "Ginny, where are you?" Muffled noises were coming from Ginny's bed. I looked a little closer and saw that Ginny was in the bed, and she couldn't get out!

It seems to me that with Alzheimer's disease, some of your best traits become your worst. Mom was a very organized cleaning machine. If Mom didn't know where things went, she invented a place for them. Anything and everything had a place. If you left anything out-- like the TV remote, the portable phone, your cell phone or just about anything-- you might never see it again. If you did see it again, it might not be for a year or two. Just the other day, I found a window crank that has been missing for a year in one of my coat pockets.

Well, Ginny and I did not take after Mom in this respect. We are clean, but you might say that we are on the messy side of clean. Mom always had a problem with our messiness. When we were younger, she would straighten our homes whenever she visited. After we all moved into the same house, things got a little tense at times. Mom would put things away for us, and we could never find them.

As her disease progressed, she continued to straighten up, although it became a bigger problem. You would look for the remote to the TV and might find it in the oven. The telephone might be in the silverware drawer. The milk could be in the cupboard and the cereal in the fridge. Things disappeared. Some things we found right away, and some are still missing. She would get the watering can, fill it up and water all the plants whether they were living or artificial. If Ginny was outside working in the yard, Mom would be outside with her. Mom would get the broom and away she'd go. Sweeping the driveway till every speck of dirt was gone. On occasion this would lead her to the street, where she would sweep the street.

Over the past several years, Mom has forgotten that she lives with us. Sometimes she would say, "I want to go home now." We always told her, "This is your home." "No, it is not. I don't live here," was always her response.

Sometimes while sitting in our family room, Mom would look around as if she had never been there before. If you asked her if anything was wrong, she would look at you rather blankly and say, "This is a really nice place" as if she has never seen it before.

Mom ready to go out with the girls

Mom also began repeating words and sayings constantly. If we had company and everyone was talking she would want to talk too, even though her vocabulary was becoming very limited. Mom would repeat the same sentence over and over. "You're pretty." "I want to go home." "You're my best friend." "Let's go now." If she said it once, she would say it a hundred times.

One evening, my business partner, Jason Johnstad, and his wife, Kylie, came to my home for a visit. I don't think Kylie or Jason had ever been around an Alzheimer's patient for any length of time. Kylie was amazed at the amount of times Mom would say the same thing over and over. "Let's go home." "Who are you?" "You are so pretty." Mom repeated these same phrases over and over again. Weeks later, Kylie mentioned that she really did not realize the amount of patience you must need to listen to the constant repeating. The strange thing is that I have been around Mom so much I don't even notice.

One weekend, our friend Nancy Miller from Kansas City was visiting. Nancy sells beauty products. We were downstairs having a beauty spa. Nancy gave Mom a birthday card. She was surprised and said "Oh for me?" Mom gently opened it and started reading. I was behind her helping her with the words. When she was finished, Mom said, "You're so nice." She neatly folded it up and put it back in the envelope. She patted it sweetly. Then she looked down at it and said, "Oh for me?" taking it out again and started the same thing over again. I just looked at Nancy and smiled.

Day Nine

Thursday, January 21, 2010

I woke up early. I did not get much sleep, as Mom was still making lots of strange noises. She was in a good mood as I got her ready for school. She was doing much better. She ate her breakfast, and her cold was better. I had dressed her in a real pretty light pink sweatshirt. She looks so pretty in pink.

I sat down to drink my coffee, and she looked at me and said, "I hate this shirt."

I have on a black sweater. This is where Mom still has a little competition with her girls. Ginny and I both wear a lot of black. I have to say it is our favorite color. Mom insisted she wanted to wear a black shirt like mine. I try to tell her how pretty she looks in pink. She was not happy. She got up from the table and went to her room. She opened her closet and would not budge until I changed her shirt. She was all dressed in her black sweatshirt and very happy. Of course, she loves me again.

The ice outside was still very bad. I got Mom into the car without much trouble.

To get the large trash container back up the driveway was going to be a real task.

I drove down the drive and stopped my car at the end of the driveway. I feel another sitcom coming. No way was I going to try to walk the can up the ice-covered driveway and into the garage. I opened my car door, hanging out the car door I pushed the can as I drove the car, stopping about every two- to-three feet so I wouldn't fall out of the car. This was a little dangerous. I did a fine job. I got the trash bin all the way up the drive and into the garage.

Off we go. I take Mom to school and I go to work.

I leave work about 4:30 p.m. to pick Mom up from school. She was in a pretty good mood. This was her last day at Wesley before going to Florida.

At the time, I thought Mom would be returning to school the first of March. Thanks to Denise and all the staff at Wesley for taking such good care of my mom. She loved going to school and never refused to go. Wesley was a blessing for Ginny and me.

When we arrived home, we ate some supper and started to get organized for the next day's trip to Florida. I put on Mom's favorite movie, *Walk the Line*. She was not jumping around, and her cough was much better. She was a really good girl.

I made Mom a bed in her chair and mine on the couch. The night went well.

Florida, here we come!

Chapter Nine – Adventures continue

Living with a parent with Alzheimer's disease has been quite an adventure. Although nothing will change the love I have for her, Mom's moods can go from happy to nasty before you even know what's happening.

When Mom is in a bad mood, I give her hugs and kisses. This will most often change her mood, and in a matter of minutes, Mom would go from saying she didn't like me to, "I love you. You're so pretty." This melts my heart.

I have come to realize physical contact like hugging can help an Alzheimer's patient's mood change. Music can also be very important to someone with Alzheimer's. Mom loves music. *You are My Sunshine* and *If You're Happy and You Know It* are two of her favorites. At the nursing home, I often hold hands with Mom and we sing. Mom does not really know the words anymore, but she does know the tune, and singing makes her very happy.

My mother was a loving mother who became the greatest friend a girl could have, and now is my sweet little girl. Just like all little girls, one day she is sweet and cute, and the next a little ornery and naughty! Even the naughty can't change my deep love for her.

Mom had a very bad fall a couple of days after we arrived in Florida. She was not so lucky this time. When she fell, she broke her hip. She had surgery to repair her hip. We were very worried that she would not survive the surgery. Mom is a very surprising lady. She not only made it out of surgery but also learned to walk with assistance. What a Lady!

Ginny or I went to the rehab center twice a day to make sure she was ok and to help her eat at meal times. She spent the next month in a Florida rehab center. Mom learned how to troll around in her wheel chair. She met lots of new people and learned to walk a little with a walker. Amazing! I was able to bring her back to Des Moines the first of March. When she left the rehab center in Florida she had lost about 30 pounds and was very frail.

When we arrived in Des Moines in March 2010, I took her to Fleur Heights Care and Rehabilitation Center for more rehab. Mom is still there. Physically, she was slowly starting to make progress, but her Alzheimer's has gotten progressively worse.

Mom has made Fleur Heights her home. She is in a wheel chair, and she is always trolling around the care center. She is up and down all the halls all day. All of the residents, nurses, aids, kitchen help, painters, and cleaning personnel know her by name. The whole staff greets her, gives her hugs and takes excellent care of her.

When Mom first went to Fleur Heights, she decided she did not want to eat. We were not sure if she was just not hungry or if she had a problem swallowing. Ginny started going to the care center every day at noon to help feed Mom lunch, and I went every night to help feed her dinner. Mom started eating again and gaining weight. Amazing!

Ginny and I are at Fleur Heights so much now that some of the residents think we work there. I get shouted at some evenings to bring someone their coffee, or a frail little voice will tell me we forgot their green beans. I have come to know most of the permanent residents. Most are very sweet, and some have very few visitors or no visitors at all. It's really sad to watch some days.

Mom had a great roommate named Sharon. She was a very kind person and kept us informed of all Mom's daily activities. Sharon moved out of state, so Mom got a new roommate named Virginia.

Virginia was a very sweet lady with some of the same conditions as Mom. When I went in to help Mom eat in the evenings, I got Mom and Virginia their chocolate shakes and sat down with them to wait for dinner. I always asked the others at the table if they wanted some coffee or ice tea. Waiting for dinner, we passed the time singing songs. We always sang *You are My Sunshine* and *If You're Happy and You Know it*. Virginia and Mom both tried to sing along. They really loved this activity. Virginia has passed on and we miss her dearly.

*Mom clapping to **You are My Sunshine***

Most generally, Mom is in a good mood. But mood swings can happen from minute to minute. She can be singing and happy one minute and nasty the next. If I can get a moment of laughter, a smile, or see a twinkle in her eye, I feel great. I know she is in there somewhere. I wonder if she will understand in her afterlife how much she was loved. Maybe someday, when we meet again, we can enjoy a good laugh about all our experiences.

Mom's stay at Fleur Heights has been a roller coaster. She has progressed very well in her physical therapy, and can walk with a walker. She sometimes forgets she can't walk without the walker, though, and tries to get out of her wheelchair. This has proven to be a dangerous thing, and Mom has had some very nasty falls. Her Alzheimer's has advanced to the final stages. She seems to have cycles of good and bad days. She can go for two or three days, and be alert, chatty, and eating quite well. Sometimes you walk in and find a completely different person.

One recent evening, I went to help her eat, and she was doing something very strange. She was trying to pour her protein shake in her food, put her silverware in her glass, and was scooping up her food to hide it in the napkin. She was grabbing other people's food off the table. I could not say or do anything to change her, and the more I tried, the more agitated she got. The CNAs told me that she had been screaming in her bed at nap time, and they could not calm her down. They had to get her up before she would calm down. I came home very upset. I was thinking, "This is it. Mom's brain is completely gone. This is going to be a long, trying time for me." I cried and worried all night. I couldn't imagine seeing her like that every day.

The next day when Ginny went to help her with lunch, Mom had changed again. She was back to being herself. She was in a good mood, and following directions pretty well and eating. Sometimes she sleeps so deeply that you are not able to wake her even for her meals. Sometimes I think she will not make it to the next day, only to find the next day she is up and at it.

Water will send Mom into a rage. Bathing her became very difficult. I'm not sure if all Alzheimer's patients are like this, but any drop of water on my mother can send her into a tail spin. Showering is always an adventure. Mom hates her bath and/or shower. Mostly, she cannot stand to have water on her face. Obviously, this is a huge problem when trying to bathe her. When it was my turn to bathe her, I just kept singing to her, *You Are My Sunshine*. Sometimes I could get her to calm down and sing with me. She always has the tune but the words are never right.

Oh, how she hates water! It turns this sweet little 4 foot 6 inch, lady into a truck driver, mouth and all. Let the screaming and cursing begin! This started at our home and has continued at Fleur Heights. When visiting on shower day, we always get the same report. Your mom can be so sweet till we get her to the shower room, and then all hell breaks loose. Staff and visitors always ask, "What are you doing to that lady?" Sometimes she can be heard out in the parking lot.

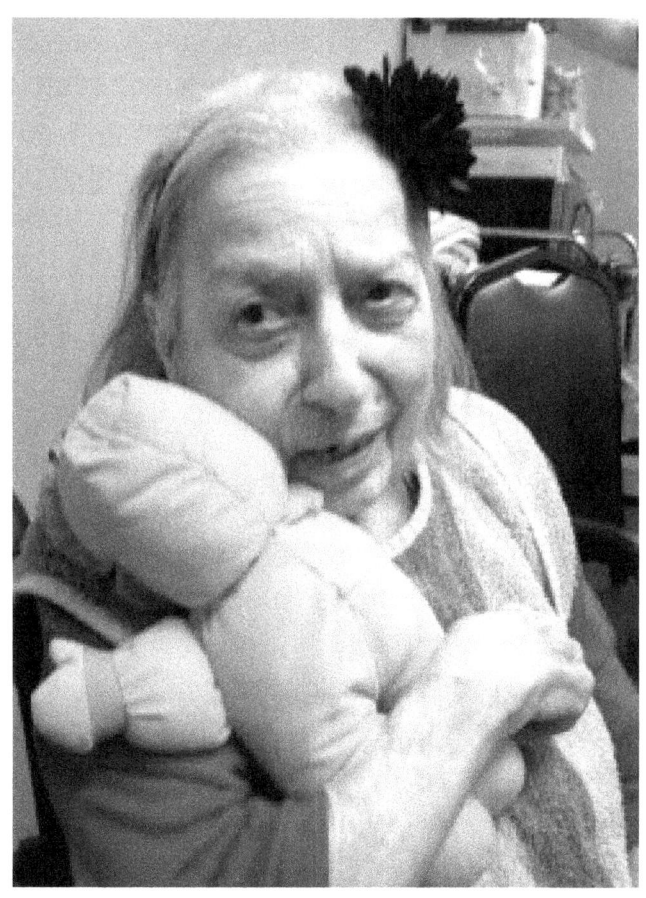

Mom with one of her babies

At Fleur Heights Care Center, she is continuing her quest for order. Mom gets in her wheelchair and off she goes, up and down the halls several times a day. I call this activity "Mom's Hall Patrol." Mom has a need to always be on the go. She stops for nothing except an occasional visit to someone else's room.

She is always straightening up and putting everything in place. However, "in place" to Mom may not be where things belong. This includes "helping" out the staff by hiding their work-related items. One evening while on patrol, Mom wandered down to the nurse's station. All the nurses were very busy with nighttime duties and had left the station for a few minutes. Mom, being helpful, went behind the station and began pulling the phone and call light cords out. She then proceeded to roll them up on a nice ball. The nurses were not too pleased with Mom's help, but they could not keep from laughing.

On occasion, she will also wander into other people's rooms and try to straighten up. Most of the staff and residents know her and are very tolerant of her interruptions, but others do not like this activity so much and tell her to leave their things alone. This has caused some very loud arguing. The staff then has to get involved to settle things. Screaming can be heard throughout the whole facility. The aides always tell us if Mom has caused any trouble. Almost always, Mom is taken to a different location to pursue a different activity.

After her noon and evening meal, Ginny or I wheel her up and down the long hallway. We stop and visit with some of the residents. Most of them go to bed around 7:00 p.m. Mom still wants to be trolling the halls, and it is very hard for me to leave her.

One evening, I decided to leave her in the kitchen with another lady resident. I bent down to give her a kiss. She looked at me and said "Don't leave me here." Pointing to the hallway, she said, "Take me to Main Street!" I took her to the hallway and away she went. I laughed all the way home. I still get a good laugh out of "Take me to Main Street!"

My dear friend, Judi Galbraith, was at Fleur Rehabilitation Center after knee surgery. Judi loves Mom, so after dinner each evening, I wheeled Mom down to Judi's room for a visit. This went on for a couple of weeks. After a few trips down the hall, Mom could find Judi's room on her own. On occasion, Judi would return to her room to find Mom there waiting for her.

Judi got well and left Fleur. One day after Judi left, Mom decided to make the trip down the hall to see Judi. Well, a man had been placed in Judi's room. Mom wheeled on down to Judi's room and the poor fellow was changing his clothes. A screaming match soon started. Mom was very upset by the naked man and started screaming, "You are the Devil! Get out of this room!" The poor fellow was stunned to see my little mom in his room. He started yelling back, "Get out of my room!" Mom started screaming again and kept calling him the Devil. The nurses had to come and redirect Mom.

She loves to be talked to and smiled at. I have found that when Mom's mood changes from good to bad, it is mostly brought on by the frustration of the unknown. If I redirect her with a hug or tell her she is a good girl, it can change her mood back to good.

Day Ten

Friday, January 22, 2010

I got up very early. 6 a.m. I could not sleep.

Mom had started to chat in her sleep, speaking some unknown language.

I cleaned up the house, did some laundry and took my shower. I got Mom up and cleaned her up real pretty, with makeup and the whole works.

I was way too organized. "What's up with that?"

I put Mom at the table for her breakfast. I go into the bathroom to finish my makeup. I keep going to check on her every two or three minutes. Everything is going great. The last time I go to check on Mom, I come out to the kitchen and Mom is eating her cereal with my beautiful black leather gloves on. Even though my gloves are covered in milk and cereal I had to laugh. Oh my, she looked so cute.

When getting up from the table, Mom fell backwards, and I kind of lost it. Oh Dear Jesus! Oh Dear Jesus! I get her up thinking OMG did she break anything? I had a very hard time picking her up. She is very upset and we both are screaming. I get her up off the floor, check her over from head to toe, and she is just fine. I kiss and hug her. A minute later she does not remember falling. Thinking back on this, I think this is when my panic attacks first started.

Before our ride to the airport came I went outside to put salt on the drive. I sure did not want another fall.

Our good friend, Sandy Thorpe, came to get us to take us to the airport. Sandy drove into the ice-covered drive at 9:30 a.m. I very carefully got Mom into the car, loaded up the wheelchair and all the rest of our things. We got to the airport, and I was told there was a one-hour flight delay. No problem. Then every hour until 3:30 p.m., we are told there was another hour delay. At 3:30 p.m., they tell us the plane is broken. They tell us we should leave and come back around 7 p.m. Please note that Mom has said at least 500 times, "Let's get out of here. I want to go home."

Dear God, is this some kind of a test? If it is, God, I'm not sure what you want. Please give me some kind of sign. What is it you want from me???

I called my friend Karen Wiles to ask if she would come to the airport pick us up. Karen is too kind. She came from West Des Moines on the icy roads to pick us up. She took us to Mezzodi's for dinner and a little happy juice. Everyone at Mezzodi's was so kind. Special thanks to the owner, Ron Giudicessi, as he was most gracious.

I called the airport and was told we weren't leaving until 8:40 p.m. Karen returns us to the airport. At 9:50 p.m., our plane loads and we leave.

It was 2:15 a.m. Saturday when we landed in St. Pete, Florida. Praise the Lord. Mom was a trooper. What a day. She did a lot better than most of the other children on the plane.

Through all of this, the question, "Why?" keeps running through my head. Again, I ask God if this is some kind of a test. I have never found out the answer to this question.

The saving grace was the next day. I was on the white sand beach in Florida and all was well. Most beautiful.

Chapter Ten – Love Stays With You

Mom turned 94 on June 3, 2012. Ginny and I were getting ready to go see Mom for her birthday, and we received a call from Fleur Heights informing us that Mom tried to make the great escape. She was all dressed up. Everyone was singing *Happy Birthday* to her and she was in a great mood. They left her in the dining room, and she followed someone to the door. Mom wears a bracelet on her wrist that sounds an alarm if she gets too close to the door. When the alarm sounded, the staff was right there to pull her back away from the door. She thought this to be really funny, laughing all the way back to the dining room.

Mom on June 3, 2012

Mom was in a great mood when we arrived. She knew Ginny's name and she called me Lou. We think she was trying to say Carmie Lou. Most of the time, she will call me Ginny. We think that because we were both there at the same time she was trying to bring up my name. She is just so darn cute.

At a party the other night, Mom's doctor, Dr. Robert Conner, a very close cousin, commented that one day while he was visiting Mom she called him Bobbie. Wow, we just never know when a little bit of memory will appear. Everyone including Dr. Bob thinks mom is amazing.

For Christmas of 2012 I decided to buy her a baby doll. She loves little babies. Well, this was the best thing ever! She has four babies and is never without one on her lap. She talks to them and rocks them. She tries to feed them, and sometimes this may include nursing. She loves her babies. Wow, she is 95 and still has the will to live. Remarkable!

In February 2014, Mom was sick for about two weeks. She had an infection that required IV antibiotics and IV fluids. The thought of having her in the hospital was too much for me. Ginny and I talked to Mom's doctor, and he agreed to let her stay at Fleur Heights Care Center since they could administer the IV. I was so relieved. Fleur Care Center is her home. She loves everyone there, and they love her. Mom did not like the needle in her arm. She was picking at the tape, and I was afraid she would pull out the needle. I had to tape her sweatshirt to her wrist to cover it. Then she was fine. Out of sight, out of mind. Mom has had to be on IV fluids about every six months for the last year and a half. This time she did not seem to be bouncing back very quickly.

The Doctor decided to remove the IV, and he arranged for St. Jude Hospice to come visit. They have been wonderful. They come and see her on a regular basis and help in her care. In a week's time, she was much better. Mom started eating, drinking, singing and playing with her baby.

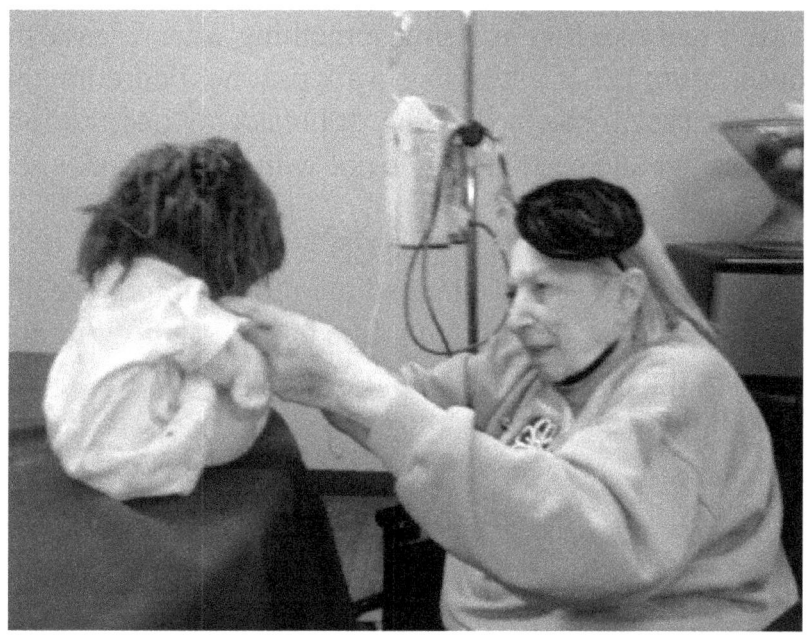

Mom and baby -- January 2014

Mom has had a great life full of love. She still is surrounded by family and friends. A day does not go by without someone inquiring about her.

When I visit Mom, her little face lights up. Mom knows I am familiar. She is so happy to see me. Then she looks at me and says, "Who are you?" This breaks my heart. My mother would have never guessed she would be the way she is.

We continue to give Mom lots of hugs and kisses. She is as beautiful as ever. Mom still greets everyone every day with a smile and one of her favorite sayings, "You are so pretty."

When I come in the house, I still expect to see Mom sitting in her red chair. In the morning when I go to work, I feel like I am missing something when I leave the house. Mom is not with me. I walk past her bedroom and look in to see if she is sleeping. It breaks my heart to look in her room and see that she is not with us. Every day, I wish Mom was here.

This disease has changed my mom's mind. I really miss the mom I grew up with. She has no memory of all the love, fun and sorrows that have gone by, but we still have all the wonderful memories.

Mom at home before her fall

What is this disease? Why *my* mom? Why do some people get cancer, suffer, and die? Why do the lucky ones just die one day? Why does anything happen in our lives? These questions test those of us who are left to live our lives without a loved one or have to watch a loved one slip away. It is a great mystery--one I hope may be answered some day. Or we may never know.

Anyone who is a caretaker of someone with Alzheimer's disease can relate to some of the things I experienced in the ten days I was home alone with Mom. Unfortunately, there are many adult children and spouses who do what I did alone *every day*. I know firsthand how hard that job is. After ten days with Mom, I had a new appreciation for my sister-- who cared for my mother alone for six *years* with only a night off now and then. Many times in my ten days, I thought of my sister and all the caretakers in the world, and how much they gave up to love and care for their parents or spouses. To have to go it alone must be even more devastating.

Still, the few weeks I spent caring for my mother was a very special time. It also was a great learning experience. I had no idea what it was like to do this job 24/7. No one can really know what a toll this disease takes on the caretakers unless they have had this humbling experience.

Being home alone with Mom was a real test for me, even though I have always had a lot of patience and love to give. I wrote this so that caretakers of Alzheimer's patients can see a little humor in their daily lives.

We never know what tomorrow will bring.
Our experiences are what make us who we are.
Live your life the best you can every day.

Cheers!

A Poem for Mary Renda

by Gina Martin

    I sit here in deep thought about Mother's Day. I love my mother more than anything, and I would not change the lives of my children. Even though I made mistakes, my children came from the best and for that I am grateful. I sit here every day thinking about the love of my life, my rock, my everything…my grandma.
    She hasn't been herself, and I feel like I have abandoned her lately. I can't bring myself to visit the nursing home. I wrote this poem so that my mother could better understand why it is so hard. I have never been able to go to a visitation or funeral, and in some ways, this is the same. I think the grandma I knew is gone and want to remember all the good. So here it is:

Alzheimer's stole my grandma away
She fades faster with every passing day
The lady that sits in the nursing home
Has a mind that just roams.
She doesn't recognize me,
Even though she can see.
My grandma has good days and bad
It makes me cry and oh, so sad
The grandma now is not from the past
Her looks are the same, but her mind's going fast

I remember all the things that we did
When I was just a little kid
I remember the twinkle in her eye
Even if it was dawn when I stopped by
 When times at home were tough to handle

I would go next door to see Grandma
There was always a candle shining bright
Into the night
To end my fear
Because Grandma was near

We would dress alike in our matching gowns
And often traveled downtown

It is so painful to see her this way
That I can't bear to stay
I see her singing to her doll
A little jealous of that bond
But think that maybe she thinks it's me
I wish I could wave a magic wand
So she could be free and back with me
Oh, my sweet grandma
How I miss thee

Please Alzheimer's – go away
We can celebrate this Mother's Day

May 11, 2014

www.ingramcontent.com/pod-product-compliance
Lightning Source LLC
Chambersburg PA
CBHW071720040426
42446CB00011B/2150